HOME SAFETY

by Lucia Raatma

THE CHILD'S WORLD®

CHANHASSEN, MINNESOTA

The Child's World

Published in the United States of America by the Child's World®
P.O. Box 326, Chanhassen, MN 55317-0326
800-599-READ
www.childsworld.com

Subject Consultant:
Bridget Clementi,
Safe Kids Coordinator,
Children's Health
Education Center,
Milwaukee, Wisconsin

Photo Credits: Cover: Denis Scott/Corbis; David Young-Wolff/PhotoEdit: 20, 22; Getty Images/Photodisc: 8 (Photomondo), 21 (Ryan McVay); Image Source/elektraVision/Picture Quest: 7, 13, 25; PhotoEdit: 16 (Tony Freeman), 23 (Babara Stitzer), 26 (Bill Aron); Photodisc/Punchstock: 9, 12 (Eyewire), 24; Picture Quest: 6 (Michael Lamotte/Cole Group/Photodisc), 11 (Siede Preis/Photodisc), 14 (Burke/Triolo/Brand X Pictures); Stockbyte/Picture Quest: 5, 10; Stockbyte/Punchstock: 25, 27; SW Productions/Brand X Pictures/Picture Quest: 18, 19.

The Child's World®: Mary Berendes, Publishing Director

Editorial Directions, Inc.: E. Russell Primm, Editorial Director; Elizabeth K. Martin and Katie Marsico, Line Editors; Olivia Nellums, Editorial Assistant; Susan Hindman, Copy Editor; Susan Ashley, Proofreader; Peter Garnham, Fact Checker; Tim Griffin/IndexServ, Indexer; Elizabeth K. Martin and Matthew Messbarger, Photo Researchers and Selectors

Library of Congress Cataloging-in-Publication Data
Raatma, Lucia.
  Home safety / by Lucia Raatma.
    p. cm.—(Living well)
  Includes index.
  Contents: Why is home safety important?—What dangers are in the home?—What should you know about fire?—How can you stay safe on the internet?—What should you remember about strangers?—What should you do in an emergency?
  ISBN 1-59296-088-X (Library Bound : alk. paper)
  1. Home accidents—Prevention—Juvenile literature.
  [1. Safety. 2. Accidents.] I. Title. II. Series: Living well (Child's World (Firm))
TX150.R32 2003
640'.0289—dc21   2003006287

TABLE OF CONTENTS

CHAPTER ONE

THE BIRTHDAY SURPRISE

Mark and his dad were busy in the kitchen, working on a surprise. It was Mark's mom's birthday, so they were making a delicious lunch for her while she was out running errands.

Tomato sauce was simmering on the stove while water boiled in another pan for cooking the pasta. Mark stayed far away from the hot burners. Mark's dad was chopping up vegetables, and Mark wanted to help.

"This is a sharp knife, so let me do the cutting, but you can wash the lettuce for the salad," his dad said.

"Okay. Should I use the bowl on the top shelf? I can reach it if I use the step stool, so I won't climb on the counter," Mark replied.

"Sounds good," his dad answered.

Mark carefully retrieved the bowl and washed the lettuce. At one point, water from the sink splashed on the floor. Mark immediately wiped up the spill with paper towels so no one would slip on the wet surface. By the time his mom got back, lunch was ready. She was so happy, and everyone enjoyed the meal.

Your home is a special place, and you can have lots of fun there. But there are dangers in your home, too. By following a few simple rules, you and your family can stay safe.

Chopping the vegetables required using a sharp knife, so Mark's father did that job.

CHAPTER TWO

WHAT DANGERS
ARE IN THE HOME?

Your home is probably a cozy and comfortable place. You may

live in a big house, a small house, or an apartment. No matter

where you live, there are dangers you should learn to avoid.

Be careful in the kitchen. Always ask an adult for permission

to use the kitchen, and never cook without an adult's help. Stay

away from the oven,

especially if pots or pans

are being heated on top.

Keep away from sharp

knives, too. Ask adults to

do any cutting. Never

climb on chairs or counters

*Stay away from the oven when pots
and pans are heating on top!*

to reach upper shelves. It is important to always ask an adult for help in the kitchen. If you are making a meal or snack, remember to keep things neat. Wash your hands

Washing your hands often while you work in the kitchen is a good way to avoid germs.

frequently, and be sure to clean up spills.

In the bathroom, wipe up any water on the floor. Slippery floors are dangerous. Get in and out of the bathtub slowly because it can be slippery, too. Never use hair dryers or other electric items near water. If they fall in, they can shock you. Watch out for hot water. Turn water on slowly and pay attention to its **temperature.** Water that is too hot can burn you.

Be extra careful on stairways. Never run up or down stairs. Take your time and use the railing. Don't leave toys or other items on the stairs or at the bottom of the stairs. People can trip on them and fall.

Doors and windows can sometimes be dangerous. Open doors slowly, so you do not hit someone on the other side. Close doors carefully and completely. If you have little brothers or sisters, be sure that their fingers are not in the way! Do not lean out of windows or push on the screens. You could fall out. And, unless there is an **emergency,** never climb out of windows.

Make sure you open doors slowly!

Not all medicine is good for you, so you should stay out of medicine cabinets.

Stay away from bottles of cleaners and other **chemicals.** Many of these are poisonous. Never drink or eat anything in these bottles. You could get very sick.

Medicine can be good for you. But never take any medicine that isn't yours. Stay out of medicine cabinets, and take medicine only when an adult gives it to you. Every home should have a first-aid kit that contains bandages and **ointment.**

There is only one thing to say about any guns that might be in your home: Do not touch them! If your family has a gun, it should be locked up and stored out of your reach. If it is not, tell an adult you trust immediately. Do not play with guns or show them to your friends. They are not toys, and they could seriously hurt you, your family, or your friends.

Guns are not toys, and you could hurt yourself or other people if you play with them.

Electricity keeps your lights on and makes your stereo play, but it can be dangerous. Never stick toys or other items into electrical **outlets,** and don't plug more than two electrical devices into one outlet. It is also best not to use **extension cords.** If misused, electricity can cause a fire or shock you.

Is It Poison?

You may not think there is poison in your home, but there is! A poison is a chemical or other material that could harm you. For instance, many household cleansers can be poisonous. This includes detergents, foam sprays, and window cleaners. Fertilizer and other substances used in the yard can also be poisonous. Don't ever swallow these or even play with them.

Some items in your medicine cabinet can be poisonous, too. A medicine meant for adults can hurt kids. Too much of a medicine can harm you as well. Never take any medicine unless an adult gives it to you.

If you or someone else swallows something poisonous, get help right away! Call 9-1-1 or your local poison control center.

CHAPTER THREE

WHAT SHOULD
YOU KNOW ABOUT FIRE?

There are many ways to prevent fires. One important way is never

to play with matches or lighters. These items can easily start fires

that can spread quickly. If matches or lighters are left out, tell an

Let an adult know right away if matches have been left out.

adult. Another way is to be careful around candles. Lighted candles can be pretty, but you should keep your distance from them. If you are blowing them out, keep your hair and clothing out of the way.

Sometimes fires start in your home even if you have been careful. To prepare for such an emergency, plan ahead. Ask adults to place **smoke alarms** throughout your house. Be sure these alarms are tested once a month. Their batteries should be replaced twice a year, too. Keep at

Keep your distance when you are blowing out birthday candles.

It is wise to keep a fire extinguisher in the kitchen or garage.

least one fire extinguisher in your home. The kitchen and garage are good places to store them. Your family should also have at least two **escape routes** from each room of the house. Work with your family to plan these routes and to practice fire drills.

If a fire does start, get out of the home and stay out! But there are rules for getting out. If you are behind a closed door, see if there is smoke coming in at the bottom. Also feel the door and the doorknob. If you see smoke or feel heat, don't open the door! Smoke and heat mean the fire is nearby. If possible, leave the room through a window. If you can't get out through a window, block the cracks around the door with clothing, blankets, or sheets. This will keep the smoke out. If you have water, wet a towel or piece of clothing. Then hold it up to your mouth and nose. Breathing through the damp material will help protect you from smoke. Call 9-1-1 or your local emergency number if you have a phone in that room. Then stay in that room and wait for help.

Windows in city apartments often have fire escapes to help you get out in case there is a fire.

Need Help?
DIAL 911

*Call 9-1-1 or your local emergency number
to let them know if your home is on fire.*

If you do not see smoke or feel heat on the door, open the door slowly. Then get on your hands and knees and crawl to the nearest exit. Because smoke rises, you should stay as low to the ground as you can. Smoke is very dangerous, and you do not want to breathe it.

If your clothing ever catches fire, do not run! Running gives the fire more air, and that makes the fire burn faster. You should stop, drop to the ground, and roll. Rolling will also keep the fire from getting more air.

Never go back into your home during a fire. Once you are outside, you can call 9-1-1. Then wait for firefighters to arrive and put out the fire.

What Is a Fire Extinguisher?

A fire extinguisher is a metal container. It is filled with water and chemicals that can put out small fires. Fire extinguishers can put out flames before they spread.

You will find fire extinguishers in most public buildings, including schools, stores, and offices. People also keep fire extinguishers on boats and school buses. It is also a good idea to have one in your home. The kitchen is usually the best spot. A small stove fire can be put out by a fire extinguisher before it gets bigger.

It is best for an adult to use a fire extinguisher. But ask a parent or teacher to show you how an extinguisher works, just in case.

How Can You Stay Safe
on the Internet?

The Internet is great for learning. It can be fun to send **E-mail** and

chat with your friends on-line. But the Internet can also be dangerous.

Some sites are not meant for you to visit, and staying on-line too long

can keep you from doing other fun things. Talk to your parents about

rules for the Internet. The

computer should be in a

public place in the house. It

is best if your parents can be

with you while you are

exploring the Internet.

E-mailing your friends

and family is a great way to

*Using the Internet is a fun way to learn new things,
but there are certain safety rules you need to follow.*

keep in touch. But if you ever get an E-mail from a stranger, tell an adult. Some e-mails contain **links** to Internet sites. Do not click on these links without your parents' permission. Many Internet sites can be interesting to visit. You can learn about science, music, and many other subjects. You can even tour some

Always check with your parents before clicking on an Internet link someone has sent you in an E-mail.

museums on-line. But some sites are for adults only. If you find this kind of site, be sure to let an adult know.

You might enjoy talking to other kids in **chat rooms.** But some strangers in chat rooms can be dangerous. They may be adults pretending to be kids. Never give out your real name, address, or phone number to anyone on the Internet. If anyone on the Internet wants to meet you in person, tell an adult. It may be safe to meet another kid, but talk to your parents about it.

You might like visiting chat rooms, but never give out any personal information over the Internet.

CHAPTER FIVE

WHAT SHOULD YOU REMEMBER ABOUT STRANGERS?

Strangers are people you do not know. Someone from another block is probably a stranger to you, but your mom's best friend is not. Your next-door neighbor is not a stranger, but a salesperson probably is. Be sure you understand who strangers are. Talk to your parents about strangers. Make a list of adults who you can trust. These can include your parents, grandparents,

A salesperson is one example of someone you might consider a stranger.

Make sure you keep the door locked when you are home.

aunts and uncles, the parents of friends, and perhaps store-keepers in your neighborhood. When you are home, make sure your doors and windows are always locked. And be careful about opening your door to a stranger. Check with an adult in your home first. If you are home alone, be even more careful. Look through a window and speak with the door closed. Ask the person who he is. If he wants to sell you something, tell him to come back another time. If he says he needs your help, tell him to ask another person on your street. If he still wants to come inside, call 9-1-1. In these cases, you are not being mean. The person could be trying to trick you and get inside your home. You are just trying to keep yourself safe. It is important to never tell the stranger that you are home alone.

Call 9-1-1 if a stranger pressures you to let him inside your home.

CHAPTER SIX

WHAT SHOULD YOU DO IN AN EMERGENCY?

An emergency is an unexpected event. It can be dangerous and might hurt you. A fire is an emergency. So is a leak in the bathroom that floods the living room. Another emergency might be someone breaking into your home. The first thing to do in an emergency is to keep your cool. Try not to get upset.

Someone trying to break into your house is one kind of emergency.

If you call 9-1-1 during an emergency, an operator will send help to your home.

For most emergencies, find a

phone and dial 9-1-1. Be sure you

know your name, your address, and your phone

number. Tell the emergency **operator** who you are and what

the problem is. The operator will send help. If you cannot wait for help or if you cannot get to a phone, go to a neighbor and explain

what is wrong.

If the emergency is a fire, get out of your home as quickly as

possible. Then call 9-1-1 from a cell phone or from a neighbor's house.

If you are trapped in your home, try to avoid breathing in smoke.

If your house is on fire, leave immediately and try to use a cell phone to call for help.

Never be afraid to ask an adult you know for help.

Home is usually a great place to be, but there are several dangers to watch out for. Never be afraid to ask an adult you know or a store employee for help if you are scared or unsure how to do something. Remember the rules you have learned. That way your home will always be a safe one.

Glossary

chat rooms (CHAT ROOMZ) Chat rooms are places on the Internet where you can "talk" to other people without giving your name.

chemicals (KEM-uh-kuhlz) Chemicals are substances used in cleansers and other items. Some chemicals are dangerous.

E-mail (EE-mayl) E-mail is a system of sending messages from one computer to another.

emergency (i-MUR-juhn-see) An emergency is a sudden and dangerous situation. It requires immediate attention.

escape routes (ess-KAPE ROOTS) Escape routes are planned ways to leave a building in case of an emergency.

extension cords (ek-STEN-shuhn KORDS) Extension cords are electrical cords that connect appliances to a wall socket. If possible, it is best not to use them.

links (LINGKS) On the Internet, links are addresses that are highlighted. You can click on these addresses for related information.

ointment (OYNT-ment) Ointment is a type of medicine you should keep in a first-aid kit to put on burns and scrapes.

operator (OP-uh-ray-tur) An operator is someone who helps you make a phone call. An emergency operator answers when you call 9-1-1.

outlets (OUT-lets) Outlets are places where appliances and other machines can be plugged in for electricity.

smoke alarms (SMOHK uh-LARMZ) Smoke alarms, also called smoke detectors, warn you about smoke or fire by giving off a loud beep.

temperature (TEM-pur-uh-chur) The temperature of something is a measurement of how hot or cold it is.

Questions and Answers about Home Safety

If I find a gun in my home, what should I do? Don't touch it! Tell an adult right away.

If someone on the Internet asks where I live, should I tell him? No! That person may not be friendly. Tell an adult if anyone on the Internet asks for your name or address. There are chat rooms designed specially for kids. These chat rooms have adults who watch what is being said. Only go to these chat rooms.

I am home alone and the doorbell rings. The person at the door wants to use the phone. Can I let her in? No. Don't ever open the door to a stranger if you are home alone. If an adult is with you, ask permission to open the door. Even though you may want to help the person, she might be trying to trick you. Tell her to ask a neighbor. Or offer to call 9-1-1 if she has an emergency.

I am hungry and want some spaghetti. Should I wait for an adult to help me cook? Yes! It can be fun to make dinner, but always have an adult help you in the kitchen.

Helping a Friend Learn about Home Safety

▸ Tell your friend about strangers. Help her to understand the difference between people she can trust and people she should stay away from.

▸ Teach your friend about fire safety. Show him your smoke alarms and the escape routes from each room.

▸ Ask your friend over to help you and your dad bake a cake. Cooking together can be fun and is a good way to learn about kitchen safety.

▸ If a friend ever plays with matches, lighters, or a gun, leave the room right away! Find an adult immediately so the items can be locked up.

Did You Know?

▸ You should always use a potholder to remove items from an oven. Dish towels and other rags are not thick enough to keep your hands from getting burned.

▸ You and your parents should agree on a time limit for Internet use. It is important not to spend all day in front of a computer screen. Go outside, read a book, or play with your friends!

▸ Fires can start from cigarettes that are left burning. If people in your house smoke, ask them to never smoke in bed and never leave burning cigarettes unattended.

▸ Dialing 9-1-1 is the best way to get help in an emergency. You should never call 9-1-1 as a joke. Call only if you really need help.

How to Learn More about Home Safety

At the Library: Nonfiction
Chaiet, Donna, and Francine Russell. *The Safe Zone: A Kid's Guide to Personal Safety.*
New York: Morrow Junior Books, 1998.

Gutman, Bill. *Harmful to Your Health.* New York: Twenty-First Century Books, 1996.

Levete, Sarah. *Looking After Myself.* Brookfield, Conn.: Millbrook Press, 1998.

Sanders, Pete, and Steve Myers. *Personal Safety.* Brookfield, Conn.: Copper Beech Books, 1999.

Schwartz, Linda. *What Should You Do? A Kid's Guide to Tricky and Sticky Situations.*
Santa Barbara, Calif.: Learning Works, 1990.

Silverstein, Alvin, Virginia Silverstein, and Laura Silverstein Nunn. *Staying Safe.*
Danbury, Conn.: Franklin Watts, 2000.

At the Library: Fiction
Beatty, Monica Driscoll, and Christie Allan-Piper. *Fire Night!*
Santa Fe, N.M.: Health Press, 1998.

On the Web
Visit our home page for lots of links about home safety:
http://www.childsworld.com/links.html

Note to Parents, Teachers, and Librarians: We routinely verify our
Web links to make sure they're safe, active sites—so encourage your
readers to check them out!

Through the Mail or by Phone

American Red Cross National Headquarters
431 18th Street, N.W.
Washington, DC 20006
202/303-4498

National Center for Injury Prevention and Control
4770 Buford Highway, N.E.
Atlanta, GA 30341
770/488-1506

National SAFE KIDS Campaign
1301 Pennsylvania Avenue, N.W.
Suite 100
Washington, DC 20004
202/662-0600

National Safety Council
1121 Spring Lake Drive
Itasca, IL 60143
630/285-1121

The Nemours Center for Children's Health Media
Alfred I. duPont Hospital for Children
1600 Rockland Road
Wilmington, DE 19803
302/651-4046

U.S. Consumer Product Safety Commission
Washington, DC 20207
800/638-2772

Index

About the Author

Lucia Raatma received her bachelor's degree in English literature from the University of South Carolina and her master's degree in cinema studies from New York University. She has written a wide range of books for young people. When she is not researching or writing, she enjoys going to movies, practicing yoga, and spending time with her husband, their daughter, and their golden retriever. She lives in New York.